GOD MADE MARRIAGE

ITS NOT A RANDOM IDEA

WRITTEN BY

KEMI ADESOLA

God made marriage – It's not a random idea.

- Kemi Adesola

COPYRIGHT

ABOUT THE AUTHOR

Kemi Adesola is an active member of the body of Christ in the UK. She lives in Edinburgh Scotland with her husband and children.

She is into mentoring, counseling, and coaching people on how to develop their talents, potentials, and visions as they grow in a constantly changing and challenging world.

She is passionate about teaching self-confidence and a positive self-image that is derived from the true and consistent knowledge of the Bible. She likes to travel and also supports charitable events and causes.

TABLE OF CONTENTS

SYNOPSIS

Marriage has been defined as a union between two individuals, recognized legally, formally, and sociologically. It establishes certain rights and obligations between the couple.

According to the sociological definition, 'marriage is considered a stable and enduring arrangement that is supported by society'.

Marriage, which is also referred to as matrimony or wedlock, is a union between two individuals that is culturally affirming and often legally binding. This union creates and establishes boundaries in relationships and family life. The biblical recommendation for marriage is recorded as follows: "Therefore a man shall leave his father and mother and be joined to his wife, and they shall become one flesh". However, the Christian faith considers marriage as a spiritual journey and a sacrament.

Jesus Christ often refers to the church as His "bride," using the metaphor of marriage to describe the spiritual relationship between Himself and His followers. It is important to note that while these definitions help to understand the concept, marriage itself extends beyond just two individuals, and no single definition can fully encompass the depth and complexity of what marriage truly means to people.

In the old kingdoms, people married for political reasons and to strengthen kingdoms, but nowadays; love, money, fame, and other factors affect the decisions to marry.

INTRODUCTION

This book has been written after three years of research and twenty years of marriage. The topic of marriage has been around as far as the creation story because God created the first marital union between two individuals, and He released a pattern and template for generations to come.

Marriage customs and celebrations differ globally, but the goal is to unite two individuals for a purpose. Marriage customs and celebrations differ globally, but the goal is to unite two individuals for a purpose.

A careful study of Scripture establishes what the context here suggests, which is that the problem with the man's aloneness is not relational loneliness but rather that there is too great a task to be achieved; the man needs, not so much a companion or a lover (though the woman will be those) but a "helper" to work alongside him in the guarding and farming of the garden. (Christopher Ash, *Marriage:* Sex in the Service of God).

Marital relationships are heavily guided by culturally determined norms, customs, and expectations (Berscheid,1995; Fiske et al., 1998).

Marriage is an intention of God for man in the plan to dominate the earth and replenish it. Marriage is the act of two individuals publicly and officially committing to a permanent relationship. It is a union that is intended to last a lifetime, but it may end prematurely due to divorce or other circumstances. Marital partners are together for a purpose more so those who are in Christian marriages. They need to align to that purpose to avoid marital abuse. In (Revelations 22:17) the lord Jesus mentions *'the spirit and the bride'.*

Marriage is a legal agreement between two individuals who share a common vision and goal. The couple can decide to have their wedding in a registry office, licensed venue, or a place of worship. They may also choose to incorporate their religious beliefs into their ceremony.

The church represents the bride of Christ, and He is coming again for her.

Every marriage is a life project. It must have a vision that guides those who are involved in it because marriage goes beyond our earthly lives, and it changes people unknowingly, alters our circumstances, and puts us in untested and uncharted territories.

In the beginning, after creating the first woman, God established the institution of marriage. This union between a man and woman is the most fundamental human relationship in God's created world. As two individuals become one entity, a man leaves his parents to hold fast to his wife, and they become one flesh. This bond is even more fundamental than the parent-child relationship. The woman also leaves behind her father's house to establish a new family unit with her husband. Under God, their commitment to each other is the most fundamental aspect of their lives. In the beginning, after creating the first woman, God established the institution of marriage. This union between a man and woman is the most fundamental human relationship in God's created world.

"Yet, despite its promising beginning, sin entered the world. The man failed to protect the garden and let down his guard, allowing the serpent to deceive his wife. Even though the man had heard God's command directly, he listened to his wife instead and sinned against God. In this fallen and cursed world, marriage, which is the most fundamental relationship, is not without severe pains and difficulties.

Fast forward thousands of years to Jesus' words. Even though sin has invaded God's creation and often causes husbands and wives to struggle against each other, Jesus reinforces God's vision of marriage in creation: "What God has joined together, let not man separate." Sin may challenge, but it does not overturn God's original design. Marriage is made to endure sin. God intends for the two to become one and not for the one to be torn apart into two. "God calls husbands, as the men, to faithfulness where the first man failed. God calls each man to guard and protect his wife and marriage with a holy zeal — first from his sin, and then from others. Her failures are no excuse for his. And for wives, his failures are no excuse for hers. Man and woman covenant with each other for "as long as we both shall live."

Inevitably, they will sin against each other. Perhaps before the wedding day is over. Surely before the honeymoon is over. Sin will challenge the harmony of their relationship in some way. But God designed this covenant of marriage to hold them together in the hard times. Tough times are no surprise to marriage. Marriage was made for the tough times. Covenants are not mainly for easy times but for the hardest.

Be kind to one another, tenderhearted, forgiving one another, as God in Christ forgave you.

kindness is greatly underrated in many marriages because we assume the other party should feel our kindness but rather kindness is spoken, acted, and shown consistently, especially between husband and wife who may feel the impulse and temptation to be mean to each other, to lash out at that stubborn spouse whose always there and seems to make life harder. In

God's vision for marriage, however, there is no place for meanness or contempt between a husband and wife. Yes, loving corrections. Yes, hard conversations. Yes, forgiveness is requested and granted regularly, even daily but never meanness.

I believe in common courtesy and the scriptural guide of 'do unto others what you will have them do unto you.

This mystery is profound, and I am saying that it refers to Christ and the church.

We've saved the best for last. When God says that marriage is a mystery, he's not saying that it's confusing and enigmatic.

The mystery was this: Why one man and one woman, covenanted to each other if they both shall live? Why did God do it this way? Why build human society this way? The answer is that thousands of years before he sent his Son, God embedded a pointer to Jesus in the very basics of human life. From the beginning, God knew he would send his Son to save us from our sins, and he designed marriage to anticipate that — to prepare the world for the gospel of Jesus Christ.

The meaning of marriage is that Jesus has given his life for his people, his bride. The call of a husband is to lead by giving, and not taking, this shows us Jesus, who did not protect himself and his comfort but sacrificed himself for us. Jesus is the husband who does not claim special privileges but shoulders more responsibility to love his bride with affection, allegiance, and action.

Jesus's love for his church is the ultimate meaning of marriage. This is the message and drama Christians seek to live out and show to the world as we make our vows and anticipate the coming marriage supper of the Lamb. This is the story of marriage. (Desiringgod.org).

CHAPTER 1

Marriage is a Sacrament

'The bible began with a marriage and ended with a marriage'.

The sacraments are a way for us to experience the presence of Christ among us. Marriage is one of these sacraments and it is not just for the benefit of the couple, but also the community. The Catholic Church believes that when two baptized individuals get married, it becomes a sacrament. In the Old Testament, prophets saw marriage between a man and a woman as a representation of the covenant between God and his people. The lifelong and exclusive bond between a husband and wife mirrors the mutual commitment between God and his people. Paul's Letter to the Ephesians says that this union is a symbol of the relationship between Christ and the church.

Marriage is a significant step towards building deeper emotional bonds, long-lasting relationships, and creating a family. It is aimed at providing security for those involved when they remain faithful to each other. Getting married for the wrong reasons can be just as detrimental as marrying the wrong person.

When two people start to live together and blend their lives in the marital journey, dating, courtship, engagement, proposals, and wedding ceremonies are just bubbles that burst.

It is highly advisable for any couple who wishes to have a successful marriage to ensure that they share similar values and outlooks on important life matters and priorities. Both partners must have a genuine intention, goal, or reason for entering the institution of marriage so that it can withstand any challenges that may arise over time.

Agreeableness is of high importance in any marriage because we are made differently and learning to understand and accommodate others plays a vital role in any human relationship, especially marriage.

Agreeableness is a trait that measures the tendency to be kind, sympathetic, cooperative, warm, and considerate with others. A central feature of Agreeableness is the tendency to be cooperative and accommodating with other people to maintain smooth interpersonal relationships (Graziano & Tobin,2009)

Agreeableness is one of the most salient and influential personality constructs.

Agreeableness is of fundamental importance to psychological well-being, predicting mental health, positive affect, and good relations with others.

Agreeableness describes the ability to get along with others. Because it is manifest in interpersonal relations, the influence of agreeableness should be clearest in the arena of social adjustment.

Agreeableness includes attributes such as trust, altruism, kindness, affection, and other prosocial behaviors.

People who are high in agreeableness tend to be more cooperative while those low in this trait tend to be more problematic in group settings.

The marital ritual is not just for Christians.

Many people believe that marriage is a Christian institution and therefore the Bible is often referenced by people when discussing marriage. However, marriage has existed for a long time before the Bible was written by inspired men and it is the oldest form of human relationship, whether it is officially or unofficially contracted.

Adam and Eve never read the bible, we are the ones reading about them, yet God instructed them on family life, relationships, and daily interaction.

Marriage is a union that is based on a relationship. Therefore, anyone who is not good at managing relationships is at risk of failing in marriage, which can make life difficult for their partners and families, even if the marriage doesn't end in divorce. Marriage is a union that is heavily guided and protected, and its success depends more on good behavior and commitment than on love - contrary to what most people believe.

'We may choose to accept it or not, but marriage changes us.

God said that it is not good for a man to be alone and since that declaration was made, satisfaction in relationships especially marital relations has been sought by every human.

Marital satisfaction

'"Satisfaction refers to the fulfillment of one's needs or wants. In the context of marriage, satisfaction is the expectation of both partners to have their needs fulfilled. If one partner is not satisfied, then the marriage is not fulfilling its purpose for those involved. Therefore, it may be important to discuss satisfaction levels before getting married. Different cultures and geographical locations may have varying perspectives on marriage, but it is generally accepted as an institution worldwide."

part of the Created Order. For this reason, we may explore the Bible and its purpose and definition (G.W. Bromily, God and Marriage).

We will explore the main questions asked by those who want to marry. For Example: Who should introduce the topic - a man or a woman? Who demands or deserves satisfaction in a marital relationship - a man or a woman?

In his letter to Ephesians, Paul explains that the union of marriage symbolizes the relationship between Christ and the church.

Therefore, Christ's sacrifice, his relationship with the church, and his redemption of the church serve as a model for how a marriage should function. Marriage is a spiritual bond that fosters deeper emotional connections, relationships, reproduction, and permanence. Its purpose is to provide a sense of security for the faithful individuals involved.

Other frills attached to marriage including dating, Courtship, engagement, proposals, and wedding ceremonies are just bubbles that burst when two people start to live together and blend their lives in the marital journey.

Who or what is responsible for making a marriage official? A marriage becomes official when an agreement is reached by the people involved. The law of the land, religious body, customary practice, and parental consent are all part of the official process however, a couple may establish their marriage based on any or all the mentioned entities yet fail to keep their commitment to each other due to neglect, violence, or infidelity. While marriage is intended to be a lifelong commitment, humans are flawed beings and may not always adhere to this ideal. "According to the American Journal of Sociology, in a paper submitted by Arland Thornton et al.

They argue that certain factors that impact the timing of marriage and cohabitation today can be traced back to one's childhood and parental influences. Additionally, they discussed how for centuries, the church and state had more control overregulating intimate relationships and marriages, but in recent decades, individuals and couples have gained more autonomy and flexibility in defining their family lives. This newfound freedom is influencing people's personal choices and reflecting their attitudes toward decisions about singleness, relationships, cohabitation, marriage, and divorce. For instance, in many parts of Africa, it is common for a 22-year-old woman to live with her family or relatives. During this time, arrangements for her marriage may be made. However, if she were to travel to Europe and live and work in an urban area, she may face socio-economic pressures that could lead her to cohabit with someone unless she holds strong conservative values. Alternatively, she may choose to live with other women. However, her religious and family values are likely to influence her decision. The absence of parental influence and peer pressure may lead her to explore cohabitation as an easier alternative.

In (Genesis 2:15) it is stated that "The Lord God took the man and put him in the Garden of Eden to work it and keep it." This implies that a third party is necessary for the success of a marriage. It is up to everyone to decide if they want to involve the state, church, family, friends, or all the above as their third party in the marital journey.

Life Stories: let us consider one of our featured real-life stories below:

Life Story 1:

'I got married at 26 in Nigeria and I thought I married my best friend and the love of my life. Little did I know that I was setting myself up. A year and a half into the marriage, my husband started having affairs with ladies in our local church where we worship, and he worked as a musician. This broke my heart, but I kept on hoping that my husband would change but he did not.

Red Flag No. 1: your inability to find a red flag in your partner during courtship is a giant red flag or you believe you have found a soul mate. Don't ignore a major flaw which in my case was an illegitimate child that my husband had outside of wedlock before I met him. I ignored that part of his life and now it has happened to me too.

I thought the affairs my husband was having in our local church would stop but it never stopped. It came with lots of disrespect and emotional abuse. My husband was a proficient liar and a great manipulator. I was a perfect supportive wife. I would support him by paying rent and using my salary to buy groceries and pay other bills in the house even while he was heavily cheating.

Red Flag No 2: Never help a man to be a man. Allow him to do his duties! You're just a helpmeet and don't accept extra marital affairs as just a weakness, it is disrespectful to your marriage.

By the time I realized things were not going to change, the marriage was already five years old. A lot of time had been wasted, so I decided to plan my life outside of my marriage and started saving money.

A year later, my husband suggested that he should travel to the UK for a better life, and then he would invite me and my daughter to come and join him. I agreed to this plan though I knew he would continue his immoral life abroad. As soon as he left for the UK, I started making plans to relocate to Canada. I am now settled, and I am pursuing my master's degree.

Red Flag No 3: Never pause your life for any man. Achieve all you need to and do all you have to before or even after marriage.

In December 2023, it was discovered and confirmed that my husband had impregnated another woman in London who now HAS A BABY BOY.

My husband is an unrepentant sinner and adulterer. I have started divorce proceedings, and I have made plans to inform the Canadian authorities that I am no longer married to him.

Word of Advice

Don't ignore your instincts and your dreams. It's God telling you to start planning. Pray to God for the spirit of discernment and don't go back to the same bondage that once ensnared you. When God says your hour of deliverance has come, don't go back to the same bondage. I am not advocating for divorce, but it is better to stay alone rather than stay in a toxic relationship where you are not valued and appreciated'. -Lola, Canada.

Marriage and the pattern of God.

God has been using patterns since the creation of the first man until now, and even though humans have been breaking these patterns, they are still sustained by divine laws. You don't have to go to church to respect God's laws or abide by the rules of your family and society because we all have internalized moral codes. Regarding marriage, it is a common assumption that it is just between two individuals, but historically, there is enough evidence to support the argument that marriage binds many people together, sometimes even for

'Moreover, God commands the Israelites NOT to marry from a particular kind of people as we discover in some parts of the bible according to (Deuteronomy 7:2-5)

generations. The aristocrats or even monarchs enter the union knowingly and with a specific intention. Royal marriages are planned and arranged because the families believe in forming good relationships with similar families who have equal values and outlook to life.

'When the LORD your God gives them over to you, and you defeat them, then you must devote them to destruction. You shall make no covenant with them and show no mercy to them. You shall not intermarry with them, giving your daughters to their sons or taking their daughters for your sons, for they would turn away your sons from following me, to serve other gods. Then the anger of the LORD would be kindled against you, and he would destroy you quickly. But thus, shall you deal with them: you shall break down their altars and dash in pieces their pillars and chop down their Asherah poles and burn their carved images with fire.

Whenever God wants to remove loneliness and isolation from a person, He initiates a marriage union, (psalms 68:6) 'God sets the solitary in families, He brings out those who are bound into prosperity; but the rebellious dwell in a dry land'.

In order to liberate the Israelites from slavery in Egypt, a man and woman had to marry and bear a child called Moses who later became the pioneer of emancipation for the Israelite nation, even our lord Jesus Christ had to come through a couple who were planning to get married.

Marriage and personal principles

Principles are guidance codes that everyone lives by. For Religious people, these principles are informed by spiritual codes, for Christians, these codes are recorded in scriptures, (Romans 15:4). The NKJV version states that whatever things were written before were written for our learning, that we through patience and comfort of the scriptures might have hope'.

In addition to these principles, each person will rely on personal illumination for their marital journeys, marriage must come by revelation, inspiration, and illumination because for every issue on the earth, there is a spirit behind marriage, and it is the spirit of God.

Marriage must not shackle two people together but rather it must liberate the parties involved. Personal principles are good, but they must not be used as a cloak for infringing on other people's rights. Some principles will have to be adjusted if marriage will stand a chance. For example, saving money is a wise principle but when you marry and you are raising a family, it may take a while to reach your saving goal because you must feed the family.

Life story 2

Bode is a financial consultant who loves to have his money invested instead of spending it, When he eventually got married, he continued to sing this song of investment and money management which was not wrong, but it began to affect his marriage; his pregnant wife could not cook, heat the house, or use the shower because Bode was constantly checking the electricity meter to monitor her usage. This led to the marital breakdown because life became too unbearable for the wife.

Marriage counselors eventually got involved but due to personal principles of saving money and greed if I may add, Bode refused to adjust his behavior to save his marriage.

CHAPTER 2

Anger against the God of marriage

'The world cannot know what marriage is without learning it from God'-John Piper.

Marriage is a religion! We must learn the laws if we must succeed at it. Most people hate religion because it has been accused of propagating evil, suffering harshness and hatred.

Religion is like politics which is equally linked to cultures. Many perceive and understand religion from personal experiences and stories that have been told. There are terrible incidents of child exploitation and molestation that have emerged in the news and of course, people are angry at God for not doing something or destroying the perpetrators.

We forget that God gave humans free will and it is entirely up to us to use that power wisely.

Adolf Hitler decided to use his free will negatively, yet some people submitted themselves to serve him out of their free will while others rebelled, faced death, and rescued innocent souls from the tyrant. Everything rides on free will.

Human beings simply need to be governed, where you have humans, there must be a rule of government. While most of us detest religion, some people may not have survived if not for religious bodies that went in search of them.

Consider the nation of Nigeria that I originate from, for many centuries, many families were only able to educate their children through the help of missionary schools that were set up by churches and religious groups. Mary Slessor traveled from Scotland to Nigeria because she felt God called her to the assignment of loving people and she went on to stop the killing of the twin children. Without a doubt, the benefits of religion on improved family life are not erasable so why are people still angry at God?

Religion, politics, and education will always mingle and impact the sociological perception of man and society.

The socio-political aspect of human behavior can be traced back to the Bible's history. It is deeply ingrained in the process of socio-cultural evolution, which refers to the gradual change and development in human societies resulting from the accumulation of cultural knowledge over time (Lenski and Lenski, 1970).

Consider Moses, who was asked to lead a whole nation out of Egypt by Yahweh God of Israel; when they cried unto him after 430 years of slavery, I will imagine that the Israelites shouted for Joy when Moses appeared, yet He faced many resistances from his people, the Israelite and the rebellion continued way into the wilderness as they journeyed to the promised land. What was meant to be a simple exodus became a hard Chronicle.

Marriage entails leadership, and it should not be regarded as a competition between partners to determine who is stronger or wealthier. Historically, men have been given the role of leadership by God. However, due to society's changing challenges and circumstances, it has become challenging for men to comprehend and define what it means to be masculine. Should a man be nice? Tough? Soft? Militant? Romantic? Etc.

To be a man is to understand your assignment and vision.

According to Marilyn Yalom in her book – The History of the Wife, she said, and I quote.

'Law and education have certainly played major roles in transformational beliefs of the role of the normal woman and man's view or idea of masculinity'.

The generic man is confused about how to be or act like a man. Should they be gentle, bold, outspoken, or quiet? This silent disparity is affecting the relationship between men and women. We are made in the image of God and equal in His sight. Nobody is better than the other as far as I am concerned.

Jesus Christ advocates mutual respect among all creatures either male or female and He was crucified for his trouble. Many of Jesus' supporters were women.

God has developed the marital template and shown it to us, but we usually do go contrary to God's plan because we are rebellious, we want to maintain control and direct our lives by our wisdom, and we complicate matters in the process yet blame God for it and we bring the same attitude to marriage.

'Whosoever finds a wife finds a good thing and obtains favor from the lord' yet we continue to look for a sexual partner, a cook, a cleaner, a baby maker but not a wife. When it comes to marriage you are entering God's territory, it is God's rules, his game, and plan.

Marriage and providence

Providence is defined as divine guidance or care. In any religion, providence is attributed to a higher deity; the capacity of a sovereign personality to dictate the events in the life of a creation. When it comes to marriage, while providence is possible, planning and preparation come first.

Marriage goes beyond finding the right partner alone but planning to live the right life with the right person. If married life is not planned properly and prepared for well in advance, the results are usually negative, to say the least. Statistics of failed marriages are available in abundance for whoever cares to search for them.

It is believed among Christians that God knows everything, and He is perfect, we are all actors in the play He wrote before we were born, we must play our part in that divine plot knowing that God has a substitute for every part and that is why it is wrong to say there is a certain man for a particular woman or vice versa. As actors request for a change of part in a play, you can change your parts by prayer and supplication to the God of providence likewise, if you mistreat your marital partner, you can be replaced.

Marriage is a timeless union that doesn't have an expiration date. Divorce, although it separates two people, does not terminate a marriage since the foundation of marriage comes from God. Those who choose to live outside of God's will tend to find marriage to be a continuous struggle. Marriage is not a guarantee to avoid sadness, but it requires a willingness to live a life of contentment and discipleship. As a disciple, we continue to learn from the master, and in marriage, we never stop learning from God. In Ecclesiastes 4:12, the Bible states "Though one may be overpowered, two can defend themselves. A cord of three strands is not quickly broken," indicating that marriage is stronger when God is involved. Marriage is rooted in tradition and rituals, and it is often celebrated with grand festivities and banquets.

Consider the world marriage in the table below as we are considering the marital rites of seven countries from around the world:

Mexican wedding

In a Mexican wedding, several important elements make it unique and special. During the ceremony, the groom gives 13 gold coins, known as "arras", to the bride as a symbol of Jesus and his 12 disciples. After exchanging vows, a flower band, rope, or rosary called a "lazo" is wrapped around the couple's neck to signify the eternal bond of their marriage. Traditional Mexican wedding food includes tortillas, beans, and spicy rice, and the wedding cake is made with dried fruit and nuts that are soaked in rum. To add to the festive atmosphere, a mariachi band usually provides the music.

Swedish wedding

In Sweden, weddings were traditionally held during the summer months when there were around 20 hours of daylight each day. During the wedding, the bride wore a crown of myrtle leaves to symbolize her virginity. To ensure that she would never go hungry or without means, her father would place a gold coin in her right shoe and her mother would place a silver coin in her left shoe. The wedding feast, known as a Smorgasbord, would last for 72 hours.

Additionally, the groom would give the bride three gold coins: one for accepting the engagement, another for marrying him, and a third for carrying his child.

Fijian wedding

In some cultures, a man needs to offer something unusual to the father-in-law to ask for the hand of his daughter. For instance, in Fiji, a young man must present his father-in-law with the tooth of a whale as a symbol of his worthiness. However, in many other places, maintaining a healthy lifestyle and having a clear vision may be enough to impress a woman and her family.

In Kyrgyzstan, there was a tradition in the past where crying during the wedding day was considered a sign of a happy marriage. This led to parents consenting to the wedding of a girl who had been kidnapped if she would cry during the wedding. However, this practice was legally stopped in 1991.

Chinese wedding

In traditional Chinese culture, the marriage process starts with consulting an astrologer to find a favorable date for the wedding, calculated from the birth dates of the groom and bride. On the wedding day, the groom would start his journey to the bride's home, but the bridesmaids would make it challenging for him by demanding money. If he offered enough, they would allow him to enter the home. The bride would then serve tea to the groom and her parents as a ritual of their parting. After the feast, the family and friends would taunt the couple as they made their way into their chambers. The guests would try to remain inside the room where the couple was retiring if possible until the groom and his bride kicked them out. This is a unique aspect of traditional Chinese weddings.

Moroccan wedding

In Morocco, the wedding ceremony is usually held in the fall, as the harvest season ends. It occurs on a Sunday and is accompanied by a big feast due to the abundance of food. The wedding lasts for seven days, with separate parties for men and women. During the first three days, the bride undergoes traditional beautification and celebration before the marriage takes place on the fourth day. The fifth and sixth days are also filled with celebrations, with both men and women coming together on the seventh day to see the bride held up on a cushion and the groom lifted on the shoulders of the men in attendance. The newly married couple is then taken to a specially prepared room for the consummation of their marriage.

Food is an essential part of the Moroccan wedding, with chicken and fish, which are fertility symbols, being served. The guests enjoy lamb stew, beef, and chicken with spices, onions, apricots, and almonds, along with generous servings of couscous. The reception includes a zaffa or wedding march, during which the groom and bride enter with flaming swords, accompanied by dancing and music, including tambourines, zithers, and drums. In preparation for the wedding, it is customary for the bride to have a milk bath and massage for purification purposes.

Marriage is to glorify God

The key to a successful marriage is not in the abundance of food at the wedding nor the dowry but to sacrifice oneself in a Christ-like manner. This means taking the time to perform small acts of service for your partner, such as calling the insurance company, doing laundry, or running errands. These acts can be both routine and spontaneous, ranging from mundane to creative. Whether they're immediate or long-term, serving your partner in this way is essential for a happy and healthy relationship. Marriage is a covenant and there Is a secret to it.

Unfortunately, many people spend more time and resources on wedding preparations than on their actual marriage. If you ask most adults over 18 to name five books they have read on marriage, they will usually respond negatively, indicating that the knowledge and challenges of marriage are not well-known. Most online materials focus on wedding-related details such as dresses, suits, cakes, and decorations, rather than on the complexities of marriage. Even though marriage is the most divisive and controversial topic in the world after religion, its failures and problems have not deterred people from getting married every day.

Similarly, despite the criticism directed at religion, it has not disappeared. The more secular some might desire our world to become, the more it seems that many seek answers in organized religion simply because humans love rituals, and deep down, we crave a divine connection to a higher power.

Marriage and Emotional Intelligence

Emotional intelligence refers to the ability to be aware of and control one's emotions, express them effectively, and handle interpersonal relationships with wisdom and empathy. It encompasses the skills of perceiving, using, understanding, managing, and regulating emotions. Women, like men, are human beings with emotions. Our emotions are a significant part of who we are and are a gift from God that enables us to nurture and care for others. However, if left unchecked or uncontrolled, our emotional makeup can become a source of weakness rather than strength. Emotional intelligence entails continuously monitoring how our emotions impact our daily lives and the people around us. It involves training and educating our feelings, aligning them with what is most necessary and effective, rather than solely following our impulses or personal preferences.

Some people believe that our emotions are closely linked to our personality traits, and life experiences play a significant role in shaping our emotional state. Our emotions also have a profound influence on our thinking process, as the saying goes, "As a man thinketh in his heart, so is he" (Proverbs 23:7, KJV).

The key to emotional intelligence is not to eliminate emotions from our lives completely but to incorporate practical input into our decision-making process and learn to handle our emotions constructively. It involves recognizing how our feelings affect our thoughts.

Understanding how our emotions affect us and our thought processes allows us to comprehend how they impact others.

Feelings such as anger and fear can motivate us to act against unacceptable circumstances, which is positive. However, if left unchecked, these emotions can cause significant harm to ourselves and those we care about. By acknowledging and embracing our feelings, we begin to develop awareness of them. We should take the time to observe how our emotions change and how they influence our actions.

This understanding enables us to see things from their perspective and communicate in a way that they understand. These abilities contribute to higher-quality interactions and the development of stronger relationships.

Over time, we may also become aware of the dark side of emotional intelligence, where individuals manipulate or harm others by masterfully exploiting their emotions. By learning about the tactics people may use to exploit our emotions, we can acquire the necessary skills to protect ourselves.

Ultimately, the goal is simple: to make our emotions work for us rather than against us. This involves independent thinking, developing self-confidence, asking relevant and timely questions, not easily succumbing to majority opinions, making life decisions based on verified facts from reliable sources, praying before making significant choices, checking the credibility of information sources, practicing patience, and gaining a broader perspective and clarity on life issues with time.

Marriage is a commitment that lasts a lifetime and demands emotional maturity. Age is not a determinant of emotional maturity, people mature at different rates, however, which means that in marriage, the parties involved should be mature or be developing their emotional maturity. Emotional maturity is a vital ingredient for a successful marriage; it requires the ability to handle whatever life throws at you with precise and accurate wisdom. Entering a marriage without emotional maturity is a recipe for disaster.

Premarital and post-marital counseling.

The success of any marriage does not necessarily depend on counseling only. It is often observed that ignorance is the root cause of most conflicts in homes and families, leading to arguments and disputes. This can be attributed to the lack of knowledge and understanding among family members. Financial constraints are a common issue faced by many families.

However, divorce is not the solution, instead, the focus should be on finding ways to increase income. Therefore, couples seeking to get married must undergo premarital counseling to equip themselves with the necessary skills and knowledge to build a healthy and long-lasting relationship. The answer may not be in the words of the counselor but when people sit down to talk, difficult. matters are ironed out.

Life story 3: A couple in their early twenties (T and K) went for pre-marital counseling because they had chosen a wedding date.

During the counseling session, the professional asked the couple to discuss the plans that they have for childcare when the lady wants to return to work after childbirth. The young lady said the baby would go to the nursery of course! The young man, the groom shook his head in disagreement and said, 'My mother was a full-time housewife when we were growing up and I liked the idea so I have plans that my wife will do likewise' but the bride-to-be had a different idea, she wanted her baby to be taken to the nursery. Their harmony was tested during counseling, and they both realized that they had some uncommon grounds and unspoken agreements.

Marriage is a life-long commitment that requires emotional maturity. Age is not a determining factor of emotional capacity, so both parties involved must strive to develop their emotional maturity. Emotional maturity is crucial for the success of a marriage. To be successful in marriage means to handle whatever life throws at you with precise and accurate wisdom. Entering a marriage without emotional maturity is a recipe for disaster.

Every married couple mutually works in their relationships in the same way as their engagement days because neglecting to pay attention to each other is dangerous to intimacy. They must also learn not to criticize each other unduly to the point of pettiness.

Pettiness is defined as an undue concern with trivial matters, especially minor life issues that are considered irrelevant. To describe someone as petty means that they care too much about unimportant things and maybe unnecessarily unkind.

A petty person uses trivial matters as an excuse to be upset, uncooperative, childish, or stubborn to elicit a reaction.

Pettiness is a toxic attention-seeking tactic that stems from insecurity. It is an attitude that leads to bad behavior because those who display these traits are overly sensitive, opinionated, and prideful. Those who are petty are on a spiteful and vindictive mission to 'be right about everything.' Pettiness comes out especially when there is a difference in opinions. It is a divider, creating unnecessary walls and rifts. We can challenge any issue or topic, but we must not consider our opinions higher than others because it leads to pettiness. We certainly cannot insist on our way every time there is a situation; demanding our way every time is pettiness in disguise. John the Baptist, Elijah, and Micah, the wife of King David, are a few examples of people in the Bible who were petty and ended up in trouble. Pettiness will not allow you to choose your battles because you insist on winning every argument. Sometimes, silence is the greatest weapon we can use. Remember, vanity upon vanity, all is vanity.

CHAPTER 3

Secularization of the Marital life

'Whatever is popular seems right.'

The trend towards secularization has led to a more casual attitude towards marriage in modern times. As a result, people often neglect the guidance of God when it comes to relationships, choosing to do things their way instead. When things go wrong, they may even blame God for their problems. A major challenge that appears to be facing the marital institution is cohabitation.

Cohabitation is an arrangement where two people live together without being married but are in a romantic or sexually intimate relationship on a long-term or permanent basis. This practice has become increasingly common in recent times due to changing social views regarding marriage, gender roles, and religion.

As people become more focused on their own needs, they still desire a sense of security in their lives. Many people view cohabitation as combating loneliness, but it is important to recognize that humans are creatures of habit. Marriage serves as a social and cultural ritual, that is repeated through generations. Cohabitation is also a living arrangement that may result from a breakdown in a married couple's relationship, where they are forced to live in the same building without necessarily engaging in any intimate contact. Cohabitation is mainly driven by social acceptance. However, the popular notion of cohabitation being acceptable doesn't necessarily make it the right choice. The consequences of cohabitation indicate that it may not be the best idea.

One of the downsides of cohabitation is that it is an undefined relationship, wasting your time and effort. There are no legal documents to support your actions during this period. Additionally, cohabitation exposes you to the challenges of married life without the benefits of being a married couple. This can result in a higher risk of emotional damage if the relationship breaks down.

In 2002, the CDC found that for married couples the likelihood percentage of the relationship ending after five years is 20%, for unmarried cohabitators the likelihood percentage is 49%. After 10 years the likelihood percentage for the relationship to end is 33% for married couples and 62% for unmarried cohabitators. One German study found that in regions with high rates of childbirth to cohabiting parents, no negative effect is observed in cohabitation. The study states "union stability of cohabiting mothers is positively related to their prevalence."

Fast forward, 20 years later, in 2022, research has shown that there is no decline in cohabitation because urban living is very costly and most young people seeking an independent life have resorted to cohabitation to sustain their lifestyle and expenses. What most people fail to realize is that the union of a man and woman cohabiting is not only sexual but there is a merging of their souls, spirits, expectations, dreams, and aspirations like those in a marital relationship yet without the security that legal marriage offers.

Life story 4: A young lady recently shared a story with me about her colleague, Kara (not her real name) who became depressed because her boyfriend of 6 years with whom she had agreed that they would not have a baby while they cohabited and built their careers, has impregnated his ex-girlfriend, and decided to accept the baby. Moreover, they both have a joint mortgage and the guy offered to pay Kara off, for half of the mortgage so that she could move out and he could get his baby mama into the flat. What an injustice! Kara has lost her time, companionship, friendships, and self-esteem because all their friends now see them as a couple, and she is left with regrets and constant explanations as to why she is no longer with her boyfriend. Kara will need a good therapist!

The scenario described above is very common in the 21st century because young people seem to have been sold the idea that marriage is not necessary before you have sex.

Sex is dangerous outside of marriage! It can cause emotional instability and destroy self-esteem. Sex outside of marriage is the single root cause of high teenage pregnancies and sexually transmitted diseases.

The more we turn our backs on God, church, scriptures, prayer, and other godly habits, we must be ready for the impact of our decisions on our daily lives.

Marriage is about orderliness: it answers to God as every other thing in creation does. Every attempt of man to change the concept of marriage is a fruitless feat that will only result in broken people and a broken world.

Any society that rejects or speaks against marriage should be prepared for chaos on a very large scale.

According to Douglas Wilson,

'Man wants to be God, and he wants to be able to declare the way things shall be, and then to have them be that way. He hates God and wants to replace Him and wants to replace how the way things stand fast whenever God declares them. Man wants to speak the ultimate and authoritative word'

- Douglas Wilson (Same-Sex Mirage: Phantasmagoria

"Cohabitation is an attempt to experience a romantic relationship without making a long-term commitment."

at the Altar & Some Biblical Responses)

While marriage may not solve all our problems, we mustn't create more through cohabitation because it is very easy for couples to become unaccountable, especially for children born into this kind of relationship.

Below is an excerpt from the Bethel church's statement on biblical sexuality.

Bethel Church's Beliefs on Biblical Sexuality. This much is clear: we cannot and should not try to "get ourselves together" before we come to Christ—including in our sexuality, which is becoming more confusing than ever before. Jesus is looking for you as one looks for a lost son or daughter. Let Him find you.

Fall into His arms. His love is fierce and trustworthy. Let Him redeem, restore, and define you. We bring ourselves, our sin, pain, confidence, preferences, and ideals to Him—the whole tangled ball—and He begins the process of transformation.

Everyone who walks with Christ has been where you are, looking for faithful love and lasting truth. Our story is this: while we didn't want or like God, He reached for us and saved us. He is our King and Centre, whose desire is that we experience the beauty, joy, and fullness of all that life in Him has to offer. We are happy to be His people and we gladly owe Him our lives.

The Church Hasn't Consistently Represented Christ Well

For those who identify as LGBTQ, we want you to experience the love of God and our love expressed in honor, compassion, respect, and safety. We deeply regret that throughout history, both secular society and the Church at large have often participated in, been silent about, or purposefully ignored significant injustices against those who identify as LGBTQ. In any area where we, or our predecessors, have participated in such behavior, turned a blind eye, or failed to speak up on behalf of your safety, dignity, and justice, we ask for forgiveness—and seek to be a better example of God's love.

You are beloved by the Lord. The pain, trauma, and injustices you've experienced matter to Him and us. In both our private conversations and public discourse, we want to express the loving kindness that God has for all people. Though we may disagree on what is best for individuals and society, and are often at odds over pieces of legislation, those who identify as LGBTQ can rightly expect that you are important and valuable to us. Wherever we can be faithful to our convictions and still find common ground, that is our desire.

Scripture contains the Meaning of Life

The Bible is an identity book. It tells us who God is, who we are, and what our purpose is. We believe that the God of the Bible is a good and loving Father who wants the very best for humanity—and He is that best. As His sons and daughters, we are created to live in a deeply satisfying and loving connection with God and others. In the beginning, humanity rebelled against Him and became both victims and perpetrators of sin; no one was safe from each other, and we couldn't stop the ongoing destruction of our rebellion. But God had a plan to heal creation through His self-giving love. "For God so loved the world that He gave His one and only Son, that whoever believes in Him shall not perish but have eternal life. For God did not send His Son into the world to condemn the world, but to save the world through Him," (John 3:16-17, NIV).

We have been saved by God's grace, which is His unearned love for us and power to transform us. As we put our trust in Jesus, we die to self and become alive in Christ (Rom. 6:4). Believers are a new creation (2 Cor. 5:17)—a new person with a new identity, on a journey of becoming more and more like Him (2 Cor. 3:18). By definition, a Christian is someone who is no better, or deserving than anyone else, who has been rescued from sin and its consequences by being washed (cleansed from sin and shame), sanctified (set apart from sin and shame and to the Lord), and justified (declared righteous by God)—all through Christ's death and resurrection and the power and presence of the Holy Spirit dwelling within us (1 Cor. 6:9-11). Knowing and being known by God in Christ is the meaning of life.

Male and Female Are Fundamental and Essential Distinctions

From the very beginning, God has been socializing humanity, teaching us who we are, what our role is, and how to be just and good like Him. When He created the ancient society of the Jewish people, He gave them essential moral obligations concerning how to treat Him and each other—a foundation that would teach them to protect and thereby empower one another to thrive. Jesus interpreted and clarified the teachings of the Old Testament, and His instruction went beyond our actions to the very posture of our hearts. He taught us how to love God, ourselves, our neighbors, our bodies, and even our enemies. We seek to ground our standards and view of humanity and sexuality in God, the teaching, death, and resurrection of Jesus, and the clarity of Scripture.

God, who according to Scripture is not a sexual being, revealed that He intentionally created humanity "in His image, in the image of God He created him; male and female He created them" (Gen. 1:27 NIV). The different, yet necessary and complementary natures of masculinity and femininity were necessary to reveal something about the nature of God. The egalitarian, non-hierarchical, communal necessity of the other beautifully illustrates the reality of God as one complex being—Son, Father, and Holy Spirit.

Though men's and women's bodies are highly similar in their various biological systems (like nervous, circulatory, digestive, etc.), men and women are different. Every nucleated cell—trillions of them in a human body—contains either a male or female sex chromosome set. Amazingly, every system of the male and female body functions perfectly and effectively independent of the other—except our reproductive systems. A man and a woman are essential to have children. Our "gender"—derived from the root "gen," like the words generate, progeny, and genitals—points to our procreative organs. Male and female bodies have been created in such a way that future generations depend upon how our bodies complement each other. We therefore do not look to our desires, attractions, experiences, or inner world to find identity as male or female as a starting point; we look at biology. One may not like the starting point or may wish it was different, but our chromosomal reality and anatomy at birth—which are not merely assigned but observed and scientifically provable—are defining.

As an example, except for intersex anomalies (disorders of sexual development), one's inborn biology is the place where every proposed reassignment surgery begins as it moves toward the desired result. No matter how many definitions are added to human identity, they are all variants, responses, or reactions to the two sexes. To articulate reality in other ways does not change this fundamental truth. Subjective viewpoints on gender fracture our ability to connect and communicate with one another and distort how we socialize with our children. We believe that God knew exactly what He was doing when He created our sexuality and called it good. We seek to live in full agreement with His original design while advocating for respectful and excellent medical and emotional healthcare as appropriate for the very small fraction of people born with disorders of sexual development and their parents.

Our Bodies Are for the Lord and the Lord Is for Our Bodies

God loves and values the human body. Not only did He design us male or female, but the incarnation (when God in Christ became flesh and blood) shows us that the body is central to the Lord's plan for creation. While never ceasing to be God, Jesus came to us as a human to present a living picture of God's image and will for humanity. And so, the incarnation powerfully tells us that God cherishes our physical bodies—enough that He would reveal Himself through one. Through the Cross and resurrection, Jesus' physical experience of life made a way for the restoration and healing of our physical bodies (Isa. 53). The Lord's Supper (called communion or the Eucharist) is a celebration of Christ giving His body for our transformation.

The believer's body is a temple of the Holy Spirit (1 Cor. 6:19), who brings healing, instruction, and communion with God. Paul rejected the popular idea in his day that the body wasn't a factor in spiritual wholeness so one could do whatever he or she wanted, or that it was a shameful hindrance to a desire to be pure. Just the opposite: the body is instrumental in our growth and maturity (1 Cor. 9:26-27), and we are destined to receive a glorified body upon our resurrection. Paul said it this way: "The body is…for the Lord, and the Lord for the body" (1 Cor. 6:13 NIV). Our bodies are a beautiful way of experiencing the Lord and glorifying Him. Through the incarnation and resurrection, Jesus has redeemed our body, soul, and spirit as an integrated whole that enables us to know God, others, and ourselves, and ultimately reveal and glorify Him.

Scripture Tells Us How to Think and Behave as Sexual Beings

Sex and sin are not synonymous. God made us sexual beings before sin was a factor. This was the blessing that He called "very good" (Gen. 1:31 NIV) and He has given us boundaries about how to express ourselves sexually. The Bible consistently addresses the complexity of our sexuality because of our sins. God knows that the development of our sexuality is dependent on our family, community, and culture. Human sexuality has few natural limitations; one may act sexually with anyone or anything and in any setting if we are not socialized about what is healthy and expected. Knowing this, God has taught us His values.

As a model for all of humanity, God socialized Israel in the proper and healthy expression of sex. Just as with any other pleasure in life, like rest, work, eating, or alcohol, sex can be wonderful or destructive. He had to teach Israel that sex with one's parents or children wasn't acceptable, nor was sex with someone else's spouse, sex with the same gender, sex for sale, sex in ritual worship, sex outside of marriage, sex with animals, sex in a group, and forcing sex on another—all were unacceptable to God, no matter how tempting or desirable. As we read this list, we may feel we have already embraced most of the Lord's ways or naturally complied with many of these boundaries, but they are all values we have learned. Humans didn't invent these guidelines in an evolutionary process or by imagining their ideal experience; rather they came from divine revelation. God taught us how to socialize with one another and steward the gift of sex to create healthy people and societies.

The refusal to acknowledge and honor God leads to disconnection from reality. The lie that He doesn't exist, can't be known, has no rightful demands on us, and/or that we are not accountable to God creates a web of untruth in society as we invent new meanings for life and vie for power and pleasure. Our thoughts, emotions, and will become distorted and unreliable guides in such a way that we worship created things rather than worshipping the Creator (Rom. 1:25).

God deeply values freedom because it is part of being made in His image and is necessary if we are to truly love and become like Christ. Worshipping things other than God eventually leads to lust—the enshrinement of desire as the focus of life—and it is idolatry. Eventually, lust enslaves people as they define themselves predominantly by their desires rather than God's heart and purpose. Instead of consistently intervening, He will allow individuals and societies to stubbornly experience sin's damaging effects—even to the point where it distorts their humanity (Rom. 1:24). God takes the gifts of free will and love very seriously and will not coerce devotion.

The multitude of possible gender identities and the normalization of same-sex sexual behavior points to a society that has abandoned the desire to accurately define and socialize humanity as a reflection of God's image—humanity created as male and female, alike but different, who produce offspring of like kind (Gen. 1:26-28). They have suppressed and distorted something built into the fabric of creation, and this is not healthy (Rom. 1:21-23). For the sake of respect and communication throughout this statement, we have referenced "LGBTQ"; but these labels merely describe a subjective and often fluid experience that belies the objective truth of our male and female biology.

Jesus Speaks to Questions on Sex, Gender, Singleness, and Marriage

Jesus teaches His followers a sexual ethic that is fundamentally different from modern society—that we are more than our desires, questioning, or attractions. In Matthew 19:4-6 NIV, He reaffirmed the Genesis 1 view of sex, gender, and marriage:

"Haven't you read," He replied, "that at the beginning the Creator 'made them male and female,' and said, 'For this reason, a man will leave his father and mother and be united to his wife, and the two will become one flesh'? So, they are no longer two, but one flesh. Therefore, what God has joined together, let no one separate."

Twice Jesus added "two" to His quote from (Genesis 2:24), emphasizing the truth that marriage was always intended to be a lifetime covenant between one man and one woman, and the only context in which sexual behavior is blessed. (He was arguing against divorce and remarriage in the passage.) The only other path Jesus advocated was to remain single and celibate (Mat. 19:10-12). Jesus believed this to be a calling, knowing that most would marry. Paul speaks of a gift (a grace from God) to be married or single. Jesus and Paul themselves were both fulfilled, celibate, sexual beings who lived in deep connection with others and "raised" families of believers (Mat. 12:46-50; 1 Cor. 4:15).

Even more profoundly, Jesus expected His followers to not cultivate lust (Mat. 5:28)—to not treat themselves and others as less than human or mere objects of sexual gratification. We monetize and normalize lust; He forbade it. Desire is normal and healthy; lust is self-medicating and destructive. Lust's manifestations—human trafficking, porn, the "hook-up" culture, and more—destroy respect, intimacy, and bonding. Other people are seen as something to be collected, possessed, consumed, and discarded. But Jesus is creating an extended family of nobility and safety, where people resist sexualizing each other, where they protect each other, and where sex is a part of life but not the meaning or the center of it. Current culture—built on self, money, and power—may not embrace this, but believers choose every day to trust and follow Him as He changes us and the world one person at a time.

We acknowledge that we and the greater global Church have often failed to live up to this standard and follow the heart and teaching of Jesus in creating safe and noble communities. The Church has often behaved hypocritically or acted as though none of us fail or struggle in these areas, and we seek forgiveness and grace to grow and embrace the standard Christ has called us to.

Freedom with Jesus

Jesus consistently saw the beauty and worth in people, regardless of how society, religious elites, and influencers perceived them. His words instilled an awareness of personal dignity and self-worth that caused people to marvel over who God was and who they were to Him. He modeled perfect love and unflinching truth.

To the humble He was kind, to the proud He was fierce; He did whatever love demanded to move the human heart to think like God does. His compassion, truth, death, and resurrection changed the world. No one was more loving and kinder than Jesus. He had people in process around Him and wasn't intimidated by their histories or ongoing struggles. He never required people to have it all together to follow Him, and He knew that His followers would take time to grow and become more like Him along the way. His grace draws us into a new way of living, sometimes all at once and other times, step-by-step.

As Christians, we spend our entire lives discovering the beauty of Jesus, increasingly finding that no cost is too great to be fully engaged in His presence. We learn to surrender and grow, prioritizing connection to Him. Even though we face challenges and temptations, God promises to help us overcome them if we will trust and keep following Him (1 Cor. 10:13).

Some people experience same-sex attraction and gender dysphoria, including some in our church community—not because they were "born that way," but because they were born human into a fallen world, and because society has disrupted and confused how we teach children who they are. But we remind ourselves that human beings are more than their socialization and desires. We need to remember that these are not new issues. Paul had to teach new Gentile believers of the Roman empire a radically different sexual identity and ethic than the dehumanizing one of their societies. As we are learning Jesus' ethics, we may stumble, but we do not reach for shame, punishment, or self-condemnation. Instead, we reach for grace because He is faithful and experiences temptation just as we do (Heb. 4:15). In all areas of life, we are on a journey of giving our whole lives to Jesus—our victories and failures—so that we can walk in His freedom, hope, and peace. We trade in the old labels and identities that we have applied to ourselves and joyfully receive a new identity as His sons or daughters (John 1:12).

We believe that God designed us with free will and deeply values our ability to respond to His invitation.

Jesus never forced people to follow Him or punished them with change but invited them to enter a new way of life. As His followers, we are called to treat all people in the same way, with the utmost respect, dignity, compassion, and love, even while adamantly disagreeing with them. We therefore reject all forms of physical violence, force, manipulation, shame, or humiliation in any kind of therapy as ineffective and abusive. These are remnants of what the Bible condemns as "self-made religion…and severity to the body," yet they "are of no value in stopping the indulgence of the flesh," (Col. 2:23 ESV).

Let us come to Him together as one unified body and celebrate the Lord's unfolding redemption by declaring together, "Your kingdom come, your will be done, on earth as it is in heaven" (Mat. 6:10 NIV).

CHAPTER 4

The goldilocks years of marriage- (28-32)

'To everything in life, there is a season".

Marriage is a unique and special relationship that was created by God. His blessings allow a husband and wife to love and support each other, share the responsibility of raising children, and welcome Jesus Christ to be a part of their lives. It is a serious, public, and life-long agreement between a man and a woman, which is declared and celebrated in the presence of God.

Determining the best age for marriage is subjective and varies based on multiple factors. However, living statistics suggest that certain ages and stages may be more favorable for a successful marital relationship. Both getting married too young or waiting too long can lead to issues. Recent research indicates that divorce trends are influenced by various factors, and it's crucial to consider them before deciding on marriage.

As the world is changing, it's important to ask whether your marriage could be at risk before it even begins.

"The ideal age to get married, referred to as the goldilocks years of marriage, it is popularly believed that the least likelihood of divorce in marriage in the first five years, is 28 to 32," says Carrie Krawiec, a marriage and family therapist at Birmingham Maple Clinic in Troy, Michigan. "Called the 'Goldilocks theory,' the idea is that people at this age are not too old and not too young."

Krawiec explains that people should be "old enough" to understand the difference between true compatibility and puppy love, yet "young enough" that they're not set in their ways and unwilling to adjust habits and lifestyle, at least wait until their brain stops growing.

"There is a certain maturity level that a person reaches where they will likely succeed in their marriage, and it usually happens after the age of 25," says Alicia Taverner.

In my practice, I see couples who are on the verge of divorce. they married before they found themselves and before they had the experiences that come with the 'singledom' of your 20s."

The development of the brain's frontal lobe, responsible for moral and ethical behavior, can continue until age 25 or even 30. Life decisions made before this age can be problematic. However, couples who marry too late might face economic challenges and money troubles can trigger divorce. According to a study by the Institute for Family Studies, couples who marry in their 30s tend to have a more secure economic foundation, are more mature, and are usually more educated. Each additional year of age at marriage before 32 reduces the odds of divorce by 11%. However, the odds of divorce after age 32 increase by 5% per year. This differs from previous findings, as the divorce risk for people who marry in their 30s has flattened since 2000. The research, conducted by Nicholas H. Wolfinger, a professor of family and consumer studies and adjunct professor of sociology at the University of Utah, found that the new trend held steady for almost everyone regardless of sex, race, religious tradition, sexual history, and family structure.

Single for too long?

Wolfinger's data only tracks first marriages to the age of 45, so perhaps chances aren't as dire as they seem for those who marry later in life. And our increasing lifespans are <u>creating new possibilities</u> (and dangers) for marriages in general.

However, a person's general temperament plays an integral role in marital success.

That might seem harsh, but others have described this possible <u>link between genetics and divorce</u> as well. "When they do tie the knot, their marriages are automatically at <u>high risk for divorce</u>," says Wolfinger.

More generally, however, he notes the Darwinian element at play, as people who marry later face slim pickings in "a pool of potential spouses that has been winnowed down to exclude the individuals most predisposed to succeed at matrimony."

Dallas family law attorney Jeff Anderson agrees and says, "If someone has not married before their late 30s or into their 40s, they are less likely to be willing to give the relationship the flexibility it may need to flourish."

Of course, all the data and the doomsayers in the world could easily be wrong, and love is loving no matter how old—or young—you are. "No two people are the same," says Anderson, "and I wouldn't want a couple to lose one another just because they don't think they are the right age."[i]

WHY soulmates tarry; marital delays.

Singleness is often considered a curse by some cultures. In Nigeria, where I was born, being single after the age of 30 is seen as irresponsible or a misfit. This cultural outlook on marital institutions causes embarrassment to those who remain unmarried. Most religions emphasize the importance of starting a family in their teachings, and communities and families take pride in marrying off their daughters rather than having them stay too long in their paternal family homes. This can create impatience and frustration for single women who have not yet received any marital proposals and may feel pressured to indulge in illegitimate relationships, such as polygamy or becoming a "side-chick."

Impatience can stem from pride and unbelief, frustration especially as we are unable to control what happens in our lives and we cannot force love to happen.

We are limited by our shortsightedness and not being able to see the future.

Getting married when you are too young could result in divorce, of course. But waiting too long—and it's not nearly as you might think—could be just as problematic. New research shows that divorce trends in America are changing. But can your marriage be at risk before it even begins?

God has set the rhythm and pattern for marriage, and He gave us the freedom to tweak the pattern according to our environment. That is why every marriage is different from the other.

The single life can be lonely and hard because the older people get the harder it becomes to find people to connect with and since the main need of all humans is to feel loved by the significant people in our lives, without love, life can be exceedingly hard. Love is the fundamental building block of any relationship.

CHAPTER 5
Birds of the Same Feather- the Worldview Factor

"Your view of marriage is your compass; it will lead you to your marital destination."

I strongly believe that people who share similar worldviews should marry each other. This is because our worldview greatly affects the quality of our lives. A worldview is a particular philosophy or conception of the world.

A fundamental cognitive orientation of an individual or society that encompasses their knowledge and point of view.

A collection of attitudes, values, stories, and expectations about the world around us which inform our every thought and action. Everyone has a worldview. When it concerns marriage, the worldview of the individuals involved matters and must be in synergy to avoid major conflicts or incompatibility issues.

Many people think that physical attraction or attributes are enough for a successful marriage, but evidence has shown and is still showing that people tend to gravitate towards potential partners who share a similar worldview. This means that worldviews are carried into the marriage.

God has a plan for the world, and He has hidden that plan in the institution of marriage to create and maintain order.

Marriage is an institution where personal rights are submitted willingly to the other party; it is not for the prideful nor for those who want to uphold social justice. The marital union is meant to be a haven, not a battlefield.

The deepest marital happiness comes through self-denial, humility, unselfishness, patience, kindness, and the crucifixion of our *me* mentality. Ultimately, the wise Christian couple pursuing a happy, God-glorifying union will model their marriage on Christ and him crucified.

One of Jesus' most revolutionary teachings was about the standard of marriage. He believed that we should not settle for anything less than the original purpose of God for marriage, which is to alleviate loneliness and propagate fruitfulness.

The power of the lineage

Ladies have been known to marry someone who is similar in the behavior of their father, and men likewise take wives who bear the same similarities or characteristics to their mother. Nobody can explain this phenomenon, but This means that if we're not careful, we may end up repeating the pattern of our parents' marriage, good or bad.

However, if we desire a better marital life than our parents, there are certain things we can do. First, being a Christian or born again does not guarantee that you will avoid repeating your parents' mistakes, but the only way to break this cycle is to ask your future partner some difficult, almost uncomfortable questions.

By doing so, you'll be able to identify your partner's values, beliefs, and expectations. This will help to decide whether you share similar views on important matters and if you are both committed to building a healthy and fulfilling marriage. Remember, you have the power to shape your future, and with the right mindset and preparation, you can create a marriage that's even better than your parents.

It is important to always communicate openly with your partner and avoid making assumptions. One of the biggest threats to a happy marriage is unmet expectations. Therefore, pay attention to your partner's needs and be willing to compromise. If you find yourself feeling uneasy about something, listen to your intuition and address the issue.

Even small omissions, like forgetting a birthday gift, can be a sign of neglect. Don't hesitate to prioritize your own needs and communicate them. When in doubt, ask for clarification and double-check the details.

Forgiveness is key to a successful marriage, try to preemptively forgive your partner for any mistakes or misunderstandings that may arise.

Bible marriages (Some examples).

During biblical times, marriages were arranged by family members to benefit the individuals involved, their families, kingdoms, and God. Exploring the beauty of biblical marriages can reveal how unions were thoughtfully arranged to provide benefits not only to the individuals involved but also to their entire families. By delving into the wisdom of our ancestors, one can uncover the secrets to building a successful and fulfilling marriage.

Adam and Eve- An example of godly life cut short.

Adam and Eve are considered the first wedded couple in biblical history. They were blessed with the opportunity to enjoy the grandest aspects of life in the Garden of Eden. God's original plan was to create a perfect match between a man and a woman, despite their differences, and unite them in paradise. This was a gift of love and commitment from God. However, their perfect love story was distorted due to sin, which resulted from their disobedience.

Despite this, they are still taken as an example in most wedding ceremonies as the new couple is encouraged to keep God at the center of their celebration of love.

Abraham and Sarah – An example of godly trust in God.

Abraham and Sarah are known for their exceptional trust in God. Abraham is referred to as the "Father of Nations" in both the Old and New Testaments. The couple had been trying to have a child for a long time, but Sarah doubted God's promise to her. She felt that she couldn't have a child at her age.

To have a child, Sarah came up with a plan to use her maidservant, Hagar, as a surrogate. Although this was not the right choice, God still fulfilled His promise, and Sarah gave birth to Isaac. Despite their mistakes,

Abraham and Sarah remain the best examples of a faithful couple in the Bible.

Isaac and Rebekah- An example of godly guidance

Abraham was opposed to his son Isaac marrying a Canaanite woman. Therefore, he instructed his servant to find a wife for Isaac from among his own people. The servant was to choose the girl who offered him and his camels' water.

Rebekah was the one who fulfilled this task, and she proved to be a woman of perfection and obedience. The Lord confirmed their relationship by emphasizing the importance of kindness towards others as a key factor in their bond. Rebekah left her family to start her new married life with Isaac.

Jacob and Rachel – An example of godly labor of love.

Jacob and Rachel's love story is an inspiration of how love can be achieved after a 14-year battle. It all started with love at first sight, but Rachel's father, Laban, made a deal with Jacob. Laban agreed to let Jacob marry Rachel only if he worked for seven years. After seven years of hard work, the wedding finally happened. But on the wedding night, Jacob realized that Laban had deceived him. Instead of marrying Rachel, he was married to Leah, Rachel's older sister. Laban justified his deceit by saying that the older child should marry first. Jacob had to work for another seven years before he could finally marry Rachel. Despite the deception and sin, Jacob forgave and continued to love Rachel.

Hannah's tragedy and Elkanah's marriage is an examples of patience and miracle. Elkanah has two wives, but Hannah is barren. Peninah would always undermine Hannah, but in the end, Hannah can conceive the greatest judge of Israel, Samuel. Instead of throwing Hannah out of the marriage, Elkanah would always comfort Hannah, and that showed love despite flaws and differences.

David and Abigail- An example of godly influence.

David, a biblical figure, had multiple wives. However, his marriage to Abigail was considered special, as she was his third wife. It is believed that people who are not meant to stay in our lives are often present to teach us a lesson. In this story, Abigail plays a crucial role in preventing David from making a foolish decision. She was a wise woman who was sent by God to guide David in the right direction. This story highlights how God can provide us with the wisdom we need through other people.

King Ahasuerus and Esther – An example of godly positioning.

According to many historians, Esther's marriage to the king was considered a miracle that saved the Jewish people. Esther was able to save thousands of Jewish lives, which is a feat that cannot be accomplished by just an ordinary woman. This applies to every woman in the world today, not everyone has the power to influence a man's life, but they can certainly try. Esther's and Ahasuerus' marriage proved that with the right motives and patience, the evil plot can be stopped. The message conveyed by this story is that we should inspire people to become the best versions of themselves.

Joseph and Mary- An example of godly intervention

The marriage between Mary and Joseph is a beautiful example of forgiveness, acceptance, and true love. In a patriarchal society, Joseph had every right to reject Mary for conceiving a son that was not his. However, his love for Mary was stronger than his pride and he heeded the angel's guidance. Despite having no idea what the future held, they surrendered to God's will. According to historians, Joseph raised Jesus as his own son. This story is a reminder that commitment can sustain people through both good times and bad, and that love only grows stronger with time.

Ruth and Boaz- An example of godly love.

This couple came together by the providence of God and through their union, the ancestry of our lord Jesus Christ was preserved.

It is heartening to think that Naomi may have played a role in arranging the marriage between Ruth and Boaz. Perhaps, Naomi wanted her daughter-in-law to have a good husband who could provide the love and support she deserved after enduring the suffering of her husband's death. Ruth had devoted her life to taking care of Naomi, and she deserved a happy and fulfilling life with a caring partner.

The marriage of Boaz and Ruth produced the ancestry of Jesus Christ.

CHAPTER 6

The Hardest part of Marriage – doing the word of God

'It is not the absence of love that Kills a marriage but the absence of friendship'

Living alone simplifies life, but involving others makes it richer. Socrates, the ancient philosopher said, and I quote 'marry! If you get a good wife, you will become happy, if you get a bad one, you will become a philosopher.

There is a truth in this expression because I know a guy who is not happy with his marriage and the expression he uses constantly is 'There is no marriage in heaven'.

I usually respond to him every time that you are still on the earth and the life you are currently living in the body is heavily involved with someone else.

The success of a marriage depends on the couple's relational skills and temperament type. When two people get married, they need to be ready to manage each other's childish traits, which become more noticeable when they start living together. However, these traits are not a reason to give up on a successful marriage. The success of a marriage depends heavily on the maturity of both partners.

"The more emotionally mature person in a marriage is typically considered the smarter one. As humans, we tend to have grand expectations for marital success and sometimes we unfairly place that burden on our partners. Below are some statements that may come across as entitled, along with my responses to them.

'I thought my life would be better after I got married' – life is not a bed of roses.

'I expected my wife to be a good cook' – you can always hire a cook, it is cheaper.

'My father gave me everything I needed' Why is my husband so difficult? - compare their photographs, and you will spot the differences.

There is a popular expression during marriage ceremonies especially in the Christian version, when the couple says, 'I do' which means I have accepted the responsibility towards the person standing beside me, and I am committed to doing life with them.

After God made the first woman and entrusted this remarkable gift to the man, God instituted what we call marriage. Two people become one new entity. One man and one woman form the most fundamental human relationship in God's created world — a relationship even more fundamental than parent-child. A man will leave his father and his mother and hold fast to his wife. Under God, she is now his most fundamental commitment. So also, the woman leaves behind her father's house, to establish a new family unit with her husband. Under God, he is now her most fundamental commitment.

Yet, as promising as it begins, sin entered the world. The man failed to protect the garden. He let down his guard and allowed the serpent to have his wife's ear, and she was deceived. Then the man himself, having heard God's command firsthand, listened instead to the voice of his wife, and sinned against God. And now in this fallen and cursed world, marriage, the most fundamental relationship, is not without its severe pains and difficulties.

'So, they are no longer two but one flesh. What therefore God has joined together, let not man separate'.

Now we skip ahead thousands of years to the words of Jesus. Even though sin has invaded God's creation, and often husbands and wives tragically find themselves struggling against each other, Jesus reinforces God's vision of marriage in creation: "What God has joined together, let not man separate." Sin may challenge, but it does not overturn God's original design. Marriage is made to endure sin. God means for the two to become one, and not for the one to be torn apart into two.

God calls husbands, as the men, to faithfulness where the first man failed. God calls each man to guard and protect his wife and marriage with a holy zeal — first from his sin, and then from others. Her failures are no excuse for his. And for wives, his failures are no excuse for hers. Man and woman covenant with each other for "as long as we both shall live."

Inevitably, they will sin against each other. Perhaps before the wedding day is over. Surely before the honeymoon is over. Sin will challenge the harmony of their relationship in some way.

But God designed this covenant of marriage to hold them together in the hard times. Tough times are no surprise to marriage. Marriage was made for the tough times. Covenants are not mainly for easy times but for the hardest. Be assured that the way you treat your marital partner will affect how God treats you not because we earn his love by our works, but because our works reveal our faith and the content of our hearts.

If we are faithful in marriage only when it is pleasant or convenient, we betray the importance of God and his commands in our lives at least for those who profess to know God.

When marriage produces God's generals.

The intention of God is revealed in marriages. In several biblical examples, generals were born to couples who got together in marriage. Moses of Egypt (Exodus 2:1)

A man from the tribe of Levi married a Levite woman who later became pregnant and gave birth to a son named Moses. He was raised by the pharaoh in the palace and eventually became the pioneer of freedom for Israel. The marriage of Jochebed and Amram produced Moses and even when the king ordered all young male children to be killed Moses' mother took courage and spared her boy in the face of death. As a married couple, they were able to conceal a baby from being killed. God created humans in His image, male and female, and from the beginning, men and women were created by God with equal dignity as humans, but with glorious complementary differences. People are not essentially androgynous humans with male or female accessories added at the end. We are different in our physiology and psychology, but these differences do not make one gender better than the other. Instead, they make people better together.

After God formed man, put him in the garden, and gave him a moral vision for life in the world, He said to him, "It is not good that the man should be alone; I will make him a helper fit for him" (Genesis 2:18). Whenever a man feels like something is missing in his life and career, when money and friends cannot fill the void, marriage may be calling him.

Is God a matchmaker?

Abraham commanded his servant to find a wife for his son Isaac from his people and the servant prayed to God for guidance. Eventually, he was led to Rebekah.

Rebekah trusted the lord and travelled to a strange land to meet her husband and she started a new life.

On many, occasions, I have been asked if God prepares one special spouse for everyone to marry and my answer is NO. people decide and God would bless them, If Rebekah refused to marry Isaac, another woman would be found for him. God may plan the marriage, but the human parties must agree.

Life story 5

Liz Mc Gregor's testimony of a great marriage under God.

"By God's Grace and the encouragement of God's People….50 years and still counting!

50 years is a long time. It's a long time in any relationship but 50 years of living and loving and learning together as husband and wife is very special.

This year my husband and I celebrated 50 years of marriage. 50 amazing years of walking the journey of life together – with God, with each other, and in the company of people who love God too.

We all need other people in our lives and happily married couples are no exception. Because we all need encouragement, we all need people to show us the way, people who love us and care enough to say the hard things we often don't want to hear. The short letter that the Apostle Paul wrote to the church in Thessalonica is a beautiful example of what it means to be an encourager and an example for others to follow.

As I look back over our 50 years of marriage, I appreciate that both of us were blessed with parents who modeled for us loving marriages and provided stable family lives. They were ordinary folks facing all the ups and downs that life brought their way after World War II, but they loved God and loved each other.

As a young, newly married couple we started life in a new city with new jobs and for my husband, a postgraduate degree to complete. Before our wedding we decided to look for a church close to where we would be living and from our very first Sunday made that our home church. This community of God's people welcomed us into their hearts and homes, they disciplined us and taught us, they nurtured us, prayed for us and they cared for us. They didn't preach at us, they didn't pressure us, they simply loved us and showed us by example what it meant to have Christ at the center of a marriage and a home. Life was overly busy and stressful at that time and exhaustion seemed to be an ever-present reality.

Without being part of a church community that loved God, which took the Bible seriously, and who cared for one another, I often wonder if we would have made it through these early years of marriage.

A desire to travel and see the world was something we had often talked about doing - we think it was a God-given sense of adventure! And so, 3 years after our marriage, at the age of 24, we set off for Nigeria where my husband had taken a job as an architect. And what an adventure it was, one that God used to dramatically change the whole course of our lives. Away from all that was familiar, from everyone and everything that we had known, it would have been easy to be enamored and taken up with the excitement and the glamour of the "expat" lifestyle that was all around us. Again, we looked for and committed ourselves to a local Nigerian church and how thankful we are at that particularly tempting phase of life that older women and men of God "adopted" us, took us under their wings, and invested in us. We studied the bible together in the homes of African and Western brothers and sisters, they prayed with us, they supported us through difficult experiences, and we had fun as we shared life.

Later, we learned the value of having wise and godly mentors in our lives, significant men and women who helped guide us when we weren't sure which direction to take and when tough decisions needed to be made. Sometimes they dared to challenge us when they sensed that we had things out of balance, and we were in danger of letting go of important priorities. Some walked alongside as leadership responsibilities grew and the burdens of life and ministry weighed heavily. Some picked us up when we were down - when we were ready to give up, they stepped in, and together we were able to go on.

And now, 50 years on, it's precious friendships with family and friends that are deeply significant in our marriage. It's amusing to think about the time we spend discussing our aches and pains over coffee but what a blessing to have examples all around us of women and men who are facing life's joys and sorrows as they grow older with dignity, with courage and with perseverance.

God's word has been our anchor through thick and thin. Life verses have underpinned our marriage and to this day we remind ourselves of them....

(Isaiah 58:) The Lord will guide you always: he will satisfy your needs in a sun-scorched land and will strengthen your frame. You will be like a well-watered garden, like a spring whose waters never fail.

(Matthew 4:19) Jesus said," Come, follow me and I will send you out to fish for people."

(2 Peter 1:5-8) Make every effort to add to your faith goodness; and to goodness knowledge; and to knowledge, self-control; and to self-control, perseverance; and to perseverance, godliness; and to godliness, mutual affection; and to mutual affection, love. For if you possess these qualities in increasing

measure, they will keep you from being ineffective and unproductive in your knowledge of our Lord Jesus Christ.

Older people are sometimes asked a question on a special wedding anniversary. "What's your secret, how have you managed to stay happily married all these years?" I've heard many helpful answers to that question over the years that are worth remembering but for us, our "secret" is Jesus. We both decided to follow Jesus as children over 60 years ago and we both prayed and looked for a life partner who was following Jesus too. God answered that prayer and it is our united and unwavering commitment to live and love and learn together as followers of Jesus day by day that has been at the foundation of these 50 years of a truly blessed and happy marriage.

And so, by God's Grace and the ongoing encouragement of God's people, we celebrate our anniversary with joy and with thanksgiving.

To God be all the Glory".- Liz McGregor, Edinburgh.

CHAPTER 7

Single and Soaring, what happens after Marriage?

Marriage is simply a change in legal status and does not involve a transfer of intellect or personality. Observations conducted on married couples show a partial tendency to adjust to the temperament of marital partners, especially as women.

There seems to be a silent universal agreement signed by women that they will do everything within their power to keep the emotional balance of the home. The African woman especially is required to keep the home together emotionally, financially, and socially thereby creating a burden for the woman.

In bible days, there was a similar expectation considering Mary and Martha, cared for Jesus Christ when He visited though their husbands were not mentioned. God does not advocate that people should lose their identities after marriage but in most cases, due to family responsibilities and the demands of the home, sacrifices will be made by couples to accommodate the new life.

Why marry?

According to a recent personal survey carried out among a hundred single people, both religious and non-religious to determine why they want to marry some of their responses are listed below:

- 'I want to marry because all my friends are married'.
- 'I want to marry because I am getting older'.
- 'I want to marry because I am under pressure from my family'.
- 'I want to marry because I am in love'.
- 'I want to marry because I am tired of living alone'.

None of the above reasons are valid enough for a marriage. It is important for people to carefully consider various factors before they marry.

Marriage cannot change your personality, but it can alter your views and attitude. Marriage can rearrange our priorities and responsibilities, but it must not change our values and fundamental beliefs.

This sudden demand to change is what leads to emotional abuse in marriage, where one partner demands that the other fit into a mold that the other one creates. It is a wrong intention and plan for an individual to set out to change or request another human to change dramatically or suddenly just because they got married. Marriage is only a change of status, not a swap of brain and personality. However marital partners are to make each other accountable to reach their goals in life.

- CHOOSING MARITAL PARTNERS- A Pentecostal approach.

'We marry who we are; we choose partners as we believe.'

Who you choose in marriage speaks volumes about you. You never stop learning so see marriage as another course of learning with you being the lecturer and student. Don't just fall in love, look before you leap. A careless leap in marriage leads to a disastrous fall.

I started praying for a marital partner at the age of 16. I also started reading books about the attributes of the male gender. This year marks twenty years of marriage and the most useful help for me has been the wisdom received through the study of books.

It is widely known that there is no magical formula for a successful marriage and mate selection. However, researchers have been studying the factors that can contribute to a good marriage and prevent it from ending in divorce. Several studies have indicated that mate selection is influenced by various factors such as readiness for marriage, personal and cultural values, religious beliefs and practices, hormone levels, and socioeconomic status, rather than just a desire to commit. These factors can be shaped by historical contexts and environments. Robinson and Blanton (1993) stated that key elements of enduring marriages involve intimacy, commitment, communication, congruence, and religious faith. For some people, mutual attraction and love are the most important factors in selecting a mate. In Christian marriages, the Holy Spirit plays an essential role in success.

The way individuals relate to the Holy Spirit and the amount of liberty given to the Holy Spirit is responsible for the success of any Christian marriage.

However, marriage within the Pentecostal Church is sanctioned by covenants.

- The covenant of belief, which is a belief in the Pentecostal church that God wants Christians to be married to fellow Christians, so there must be evidence that couples have accepted Jesus Christ as their savior.

- The covenant of purity, mandates that one abstains from sexual relations until after the wedding has taken place. This covenant comes from the belief that sexual relations between men and women are intended only for the bonds of marriage.

- The need for the couple to live separately until the marriage has taken place. This is another term for the covenant of purity, as the Pentecostal church sees cohabitation before marriage as compromising to Christian witness.

- The covenant of faithfulness by agreeing to keep Christ as a central focus throughout their marriage. This includes a life based on true faith and continued participation in His church.

Finally, the couple must realize that the minister selected to marry the couple reserves the right to deny services if the minister feels that the obligations to this covenant have not been met. McKay and Quick (2005) stated that relationships are "much more effective" if individuals "use what they know about each other's needs to develop a new collaborative solution to your problem" (p. 122). They further suggest that couples must explore their expectations of each other as well as their "hopes, desires, and needs" to assist in their process of developing a committed relationship.

According to biblical texts, the union of a man and a woman symbolizes the relationship between Jesus Christ and the church. The Pentecostal teachings about marriage motivate individuals to seek a mate with the mindset to remain married "until death do us part." However, pre-marital preparation is essential to mitigate divorce, separation, and marital abuse. A failed relationship is better than a failed marriage.

When individuals begin the process of getting involved with each other romantically, it is advisable to get others involved too. For those who are Christians, avoid leaving your church family behind. We don't usually think of our church family as part of our pursuit of marriage (maybe we even cringe at the idea), but as uncomfortable or inconvenient as it may sound, God gives the primary and final responsibility of our accountability to the local church (Matthew 18:15–20; Hebrews 13:17).

God means for the church to be the rough tread on the edge of the highway, making sure we stay awake and alert while driving in life, including in dating. If we do not build our church families into our routines and our relationships, we are likely to ride right off into a spiritual or relational ditch. The church, however, can surround a couple with structure, direction, and safety.

Now, this does not mean you need to stand up during the announcements and give the whole church an update on your relationship or print a weekly update in the bulletin. But lean on fellow Christians, and especially those who are older and more mature. Allow yourself to mingle with people you would not spend time with usually and invite them into your thinking and decision-making in a mate selection. Be accountable to a local church: plug in, get to know and be known by others, seek out people different from you, and draw them into what you are thinking, wanting, and experiencing in your relationship, do not leave the church behind.

Secondly, lean into the love that made and raised you. "Honour your father and your mother" (Exodus 20:12). It is so simple, and yet it can often be challenging, and even more so in dating. In our day, it is increasingly unexpected to involve your parents at all. It seems old-fashioned and unnecessary. Parents are typically a formality once we have already made our own decisions — unless, of course, we want to listen to God and pursue marriage more wisely. Wisdom says, "Listen to your father who gave your life and does not despise your mother when she is old. . .. Let your father and mother be glad; let her who bore you rejoice" (Proverbs 23:22, 25).

We may not agree completely with our parents or our parents may not even be believers or they are divorced and disagree with each other about what we should do. Our parents may not be interested in being involved in our relationship and we cannot force our parents to care or cooperate, but we can *honour* them, and think of creative ways to encourage them to be involved and to solicit their input.

Our parents may be flat-out wrong, but most parents do not intentionally want to harm us or keep us from being happy. They have known and loved us longer than anyone else, and genuinely want what they think is best for us.

What if we loved our parents *more* intentionally and *more* joyfully when we disagreed with them? What would that say — to them, to our significant other, to the rest of our friends and family — about our faith in Jesus? Lean into the love that made and raised you.

Finally, be open to the friends who know us best and who love us and Jesus enough to hold us accountable. We do not just need friends. Everybody has friends. We need *real* friends — friends who know us well, who are regularly and actively involved in our relationship, and who love us enough to ask tough questions or tell us when we are wrong.

Even after God rescues us from our sin, pulls us out of the pit, and puts his Spirit inside of us, we still battle the remaining sin, and we are helpless on our own.

We need friends in the fight to help us see where we are wrong or weak. Do not wait for a friend to come ask you how things are going. Seek those few friends out and share openly with them. You might ask each other questions like these:

- What do the two of you talk about? What's a typical conversation like?

- How far have you gone physically, where will you draw the line, and in what situations do you experience the most temptation?

- What are you learning about him (or her)? Are you moving toward or away from clarity about marriage?

- How has your relationship affected your spiritual health, including prayer life, Bible reading, involvement in the local church, and ministry to others?

Does anyone ask you questions like these? Who are the friends who will go there with you? If you do not have them, do you know anyone who could potentially become that kind of friend? Do you know anyone who might need you to be that friend for them? (adapted from desiring god.org).

Arranged marriage.

The context of arranged marriages is different from the concept of individual freedom. Such marriages are characterized by collective dynamics, where power is distributed among family members and the community is involved. The process of arranged marriages heavily relies on parental and extended family input, which fails to meet the requirements of free and full consent. While consent is a universal principle, it cannot be fully applied in arranged marriages because the system is not primarily focused on individualism. In the discourse of arranged marriages, the language of consent is often used, which is based on individualism and autonomy. However, this language is not suitable for a system that emphasizes community belonging, duty, and purpose.

Arranged marriage cultures rely on the authority and leadership of guardians. It can be considered a rule of parental authority or an aristocratic marital system. In such a system, a minority of individuals who possess superior knowledge and virtue should be entrusted with governing. Traditionally, the elderly are the entrusted ones, and the young individuals honor their authority.

Dating wastes time! Dating wastes time!! Dating wastes time!!!

Online dating mentors often give the most bizarre because people want answers to their romantic hunger. We all seek love and companionship, but it's important to approach online dating with caution and mindfulness. Consider some of the short statements below and you will agree with me that if any single person follows this so-called advice, their life may be affected negatively. My thoughts on this advice are in brackets.

- "Keep dates short." (Why did you bother?)
- "Be upfront about wanting a relationship"- (This is desperation at its best)
- "Avoid talking about exes on early dates." (Do you have a record of their names?)

- "Do not feel obligated to send a thank-you text." (wow, signs of ingratitude)
- "Give them two weeks to reach out again." (After the show of ingratitude, I do not think so).
- "Wait at least a few dates to have sex." (still do not think so).

Final word for the ladies (men, lend us your hearts and ears).

"When marriage is concerned, there is not a pre-planned right time. When you find the right person (carefully and prayerfully), you should not delay. Not delaying has practical implications, especially when there are children involved. It is important to understand the biblical meaning of submission, it does not mean subservience, but it does require a level of sacrifice and willingness to submit your dreams (delay, suspend, pause) not necessarily give up. Be prepared for your career growth to be slower in certain seasons of your life, especially through pregnancy and maternity leave. It is important to maintain an honest and cordial communication line with your spouse. Listen to understand their ambitions and dreams then go all out to support them to achieve this while you also ensure that they know your career intentions and usually they will reciprocate with support as you have sown that too.

- Marriage is good, God is the perfect matchmaker. Do not listen to all the negative news. Prepare for marriage, read books on marriage, and attend seminars. Listen to experienced marriage speakers, pray ahead, pray for your husband even if you have not met him yet, and pray for your unborn children. Refuse to give in to fear and anxiety nor entertain pity parties, nothing is wrong with you, and do not swallow any suggestions that you are not good enough. However, do not be choosy to the point of being impossible but do not settle for what you know you cannot live with for the rest of your life. Speak to and get encouragement from other people with godly marriages you admire but do not put your life on hold. Live your life to the fullest glorifying God, and whether you marry before Jesus comes or Jesus returns before you marry do not miss the marriage feast of the lamb. (Oyebola Ajala, Motherwell, Scotland)."

CONCLUSION

The issue surrounding marriage is inexhaustible and no one apart from God can make a marriage secure. Fear is everywhere and everyone seems to panic and wonder if their marriage will succeed. We must learn to trust God daily and invite Him into our lives consciously. Marriage was His idea anyway, which means He has the prototype, I submit that marriage should not be entered into based on assumption, but parties must do their due diligence before marriage. Clarity must be sought about important facts of life and family background, finances, life after marriage, etc.

Marriage is about self-sacrifice and death for selfishness. Finding ways to serve in the marriage and thereby building a safe community. Marriage can move you towards God for the joy in it, or make you move far away from God because of the pain it may cause. God never intended for anyone to be afflicted in marriage or by marriage but our choices, desires, and misaligned hunger for satisfaction lead and bad choices lead to marital suffering. For the modern men and women, I submit to you that the rules of marriage will not change for you or any generation, whatever a man sows, he will reap! My word of advice is to begin the act of laying a good foundation now for what you intend to see in the future. Learn to give, sacrifice, pay attention to the teaching of the word of God, and obey spiritual guidance that you trust.

Until we meet at the marriage of the lamb, may God keep you in His love and give you the grace to find joy and happiness in marriage.

Kemi Adesola©2024.

REFERENCES

1. Robinson and Blanton,1993

2. Berscheid 1995, Fiske et al 1998

3. Lenski 1970

4. McKay and Quack, 2005

Recommended resources

1. Help me, I'm married- Joyce Meyer.

2. This momentary marriage- John Piper

3. The marriage covenant- Derek Prince.

4. God and Marriage – G.W Bromily

5. Same-sex Mirage – Douglas Wilson

6. The history of the wife – Marilyn Yalom

7. Desiring god.org

8. Bethel church.com

9. Understanding arranged marriage: An unbaised analysis of a traditional marital institution–Naema N Tahir

10. American journal of Sociology

OTHER BOOKS BY KEMI ADESOLA

1. Remembering Faith when plans fail.
2. The power meal
3. The follower leader
4. What happened to the church?
5. The invisible barrier.
6. The future awaits
7. How to pray and God will listen

Printed in Great Britain
by Amazon

37237655R00069